Melanie

Merry Christmas

Love Lauren

x x

Classic Kiwiana

Classic Kiwiana

An essential guide to *New Zealand* popular culture

RICHARD WOLFE   STEPHEN BARNETT

PENGUIN BOOKS

PENGUIN BOOKS
Published by the Penguin Group
Penguin Group (NZ), 67 Apollo Drive, Rosedale,
North Shore 0632, New Zealand (a division of Pearson New Zealand Ltd)
Penguin Group (USA) Inc., 375 Hudson Street,
New York, New York 10014, USA
Penguin Group (Canada), 90 Eglinton Avenue East, Suite 700, Toronto,
Ontario, M4P 2Y3, Canada (a division of Pearson Penguin Canada Inc.)
Penguin Books Ltd, 80 Strand, London, WC2R 0RL, England
Penguin Ireland, 25 St Stephen's Green
Dublin 2, Ireland (a division of Penguin Books Ltd)
Penguin Group (Australia), 250 Camberwell Road, Camberwell,
Victoria 3124, Australia (a division of Pearson Australia Group Pty Ltd)
Penguin Books India Pvt Ltd, 11, Community Centre,
Panchsheel Park, New Delhi - 110 017, India
Penguin Books (South Africa) (Pty) Ltd, 24 Sturdee Avenue,
Rosebank, Johannesburg 2196, South Africa

Penguin Books Ltd, Registered Offices: 80 Strand, London, WC2R 0RL, England

First published by Penguin Books (NZ) Ltd, 2001
This edition published 2007
10 9 8 7 6 5 4 3 2 1
Copyright © Richard Wolfe and Stephen Barnett 2001

The authors are grateful to the following for their assistance with this book:
Alexander Turnbull Library, Alliance Textiles Ltd, Bluebird Foods, Brian Chudleigh, Coca-Cola Amatil (NZ) Ltd,
Diogenes Designs Ltd, Colin Edgerly, Fotopress Ltd, Keith Lawson, Geoff Mason, NZ Dairy Foods, NZ Rugby
Museum, Sanitarium Health Foods, Paul Thompson, Tip-Top Ice Cream Co. Ltd, J. Wattie Foods Ltd.

The right of Richard Wolfe and Stephen Barnett to be identified as the authors of this work
in terms of section 96 of the Copyright Act 1994 is hereby asserted.

Designed by Studio Alexander
Typeset by Thinking Caps Visual Communications
Printed by Condor Production, Hong Kong

ISBN 978 0 14 300862 0

www.penguin.com

Contents

Wattie's

GREEN PEAS

This book celebrates the 'New Zealand difference' we know as kiwiana — those quintessential customs and artefacts this country has made its own.

Kiwiana is this country's popular culture and comprises those everyday items that are familiar to most New Zealanders, irrespective of their ethnic backgrounds. Although easily overlooked, these are the very things that help define our national identity.

Many examples of kiwiana reflect obvious aspects of our way of life, such as our enthusiasm for sport and the outdoors. Some are the work of nature, while others acknowledge the efforts of New Zealanders themselves. What all these unlikely items have in common is that they are either natural or manufactured responses to life in our remote and far-flung islands.

An important feature of much kiwiana is its modesty, in size and appearance. Number 8 wire, for example, has been essential to the national economy, both for fencing and as a symbol of local ingenuity, while corrugated iron has provided a roof over our heads for a century and a half.

What is it that makes a classic piece of kiwiana? Generally, it is time and the will of the people that decide. All these representatives have served New Zealand well, either as symbols or everyday objects. Examples include the Crown Lynn Railways cup, reflecting our peculiarly practical sense of design; and 'Dog': from Footrot Flats, representing the country's long-serving rural dependence on sheep and farming; while bungy jumping exemplifies a new adventurous national spirit.

But any list needs to be flexible, according to the nation's changing circumstances. The selection here includes several endangered items, such as the traditional no-nonsense bach by the sea, which is fast becoming a thing of the past. Even the country's national bird — and ironically the inspiration for kiwiana itself — is struggling to survive.

This collection of kiwiana gathers together some of the more colourful threads of New Zealand's national character, and may therefore explain something of life in a country that can claim 40 million sheep, four million people — and a drink that is 'world famous in New Zealand'.

RICHARD WOLFE
STEPHEN BARNETT
Auckland

A staple of school lunches and picnics is the triangular-shaped, smooth-textured, smoky-tasting cheese segment made by Chesdale. Dating back to a time when home refrigeration was a rarity, Chesdale processed cheese had the virtue of surviving in the cupboard without the need to be kept cool. Ordinary cheese would sweat, become oily, dry out, crack, grow mould and start to smell once it had been cut.

Chesdale continues to be popular today with the help of a couple of rural types, Ches and Dale, and a jingle that has become part of New Zealand folklore. Ches and Dale first appeared in the early 1960s and on television in 1965 singing the song that would later be heard around the world whenever nostalgic, patriotic Kiwis got together:

We are the boys from down on the farm,
we really know our cheese
There's much better value in Chesdale,
it never fails to please
Chesdale slices thinly, never crumbles,
there's no waste
And boy it's got a mighty taste
Chesdale cheese — it's finest cheddar,
made better!

Ches and Dale were retired from television advertising around 1975, then relaunched in recent years accompanied by a Ches Junior. These days Chesdale is available in a range of flavours, and in individually wrapped slices for easy sandwich making.

Bungy jumping, inspired by the Pentecost Islanders of Vanuatu by way of Oxford University, is a Kiwi innovation that has brought an extreme sport to mainstream popularity.

The Pentecost Island 'land-diving' custom, using vines tied around the ankles to stop the jumper coming face-to-face with the ground beneath, was picked up in the 1970s by the Oxford University Dangerous Sports Club, a group of adventurous students who travelled the world trying their hands at extreme sports and challenges, frequently while dressed in top hat and tails, and drinking champagne. Among their exploits was a bungy jump from the Golden Gate Bridge in San Francisco.

This was inspiration for New Zealander A. J. Hackett who, with Henry van Asch, would spend three years on research and development of the elastic cords and the jumping itself to perfect a system that meant anyone could jump safely. Hackett first sent Kiwis over the edge at his Queenstown site and since then has taken bungy jumping to the world.

In the years since, thousands of people, for whom life is presumably not exciting or dangerous enough, have chosen to jump from great heights at the end of an elastic cord.

Hackett's own jumps are legendary — including leaps from hot-air balloons and helicopters — with perhaps the most famous being from the Eiffel Tower in 1987, which gave a global launch to bungy jumping. Today it is recognised as a major drawcard for tourists coming to New Zealand.

New Zealand's national game first kicked off in Nelson in 1870, and during the 1880s teams toured here from New South Wales and Britain. When New Zealand's representative team went to Britain in 1905 — during which time they became known as the All Blacks — they were controversially denied a clean sweep when a try by wing-threequarter Bob Deans was disallowed by the referee. The All Blacks managed their revenge two decades later in the triumphant 1924-5 tour by the undefeated 'Invincibles', but Deans' try continues to this day to be a matter of debate between New Zealand and Welsh rugby.

For nearly a century, the game of rugby changed little; players from all walks of life would pack down together and dream of leading the All Blacks to victory over their traditional enemies — the Springboks. Your average All Black was then a farmer hailing from the back-blocks of the King Country, Wairarapa or North Canterbury — players such as Brian Lochore, the Meads brothers, and Don Clarke. And the game was then staunchly amateur; even All Blacks had to get time off work to represent their country.

But in the 1990s, rugby managed the unthinkable by embracing professionalism. Apart from making selected players extremely wealthy, it required new allegiances with the introduction of the international Super 12 competition. It became big business. Despite this, rugby remains the social glue of life in many parts of provincial New Zealand. Here, at the grassroots, is the heart and soul of rugby, where the game is played for the sheer enjoyment of it all.

The traditional symbol of rugby supremacy within New Zealand has been the Ranfurly Shield, fought over by provincial teams. In the 1970s it was joined by the NPC (National Provincial Championship) competition, a true national competition across three divisions that is supported by local loyalties as vigorously — indeed, perhaps more so — in the lower divisions than in the first.

With its moist, temperate climate, New Zealand grows grass well. So well, in fact, that the country's main export earnings are derived from the efficient conversion of that grass into meat, wool and dairy products.

In suburbia, however, with few herds or flocks to keep the grass down, the lawn is something of a preoccupation for most householders, and weekends are accompanied by the whine of two-stroke engines as motor mowers are fired up to tackle the encroaching sward.

The Masport brand of New Zealand's most famous lawn mower had its origins in 1910 when two young engineers, Reuben Porter and Harold Mason, set up in business together. After a time manufacturing farm engines, and agricultural engineering, their company launched in 1930 the first of its hand-push lawn mowers, the 'Cleveland'. Masport's first power mower was introduced eight years later. These were cylindrical mowers more suited to fine grass types than the usual lawn grasses found in this country and were mostly defeated by the coarse lawn grasses —

paspalum for one — that dominate much of Australian and New Zealand suburbia.

It would not be until an afternoon in 1952 that the face of Antipodean lawn mowing would be changed forever. It was on this day in Concorde, NSW, Australia, that Mervyn Victor Richardson connected a small petrol motor to a blade and so gave birth to the world's first rotary mower. The greater cutting power of the rotary proved an immediate hit. Richardson christened his mower the 'Victa'. New Zealand rotary mowers soon followed.

The history of New Zealand is in large part the history of its colonisation by sheep. A first tentative step for sheepkind was the liberation of a ram and a ewe by Captain Cook in 1793 in the Marlborough Sounds, but they were not to survive. Nor is it recorded as successful the release, twenty-one years later, by the Rev. Samuel Marsden of a few merinos. The first real flock of sheep, also merinos, was established on Mana Island, near Wellington, in 1834. These animals were also responsible for this country's first export of wool, and within ten years sheep farming had become a serious business.

The first sale of wool in this country was conducted on Auckland's Queen's Wharf in 1858 when 250 bales went at prices ranging from 9^1/$_2$d to 17^1/$_2$d. Thus began New Zealand's heavy dependence on wool. It would become the longest sustained export commodity in the country's history, and in the 1860s represented nearly 75 per cent of all its exports.

Wool was essential to the economy of the young colony, and it was hardly surprising that it would enrich the country in other ways. For a start, the national vocabulary would find itself enlarged with such terms as wool-baron, wool-blind, wool-book, wool-cheque, wool-classer, wool-clip, wool-handler, wool-hook, wool-pack, wool-picker, wool-press, wool-puller, wool-scourer, wool-store and wool-table, to name a few. Above all, of course, was the essential woolshed, the distinctive building, typically in red-painted corrugated iron, dedicated to the shearing of sheep and the processing and packing of fleeces. Samuel Butler described the woolshed as a roomy place, built somewhat on the same plan as a cathedral, with aisles on either side full of pens for the sheep, a great nave, at the upper end of which the shearers worked, and a further space for wool-sorters and packers.

New Zealand's sheep population is today well down from its all-time high of 70 million, achieved in 1981. While sheep have also been rather ignominiously outnumbered by the country's most successful four-legged pest, the possum, they can still claim a high profile. This is particularly true of Te Kuiti, home to a number of Golden Shears Open and New Zealand Shearing Championship winners and, therefore, self-styled shearing capital of the world.

G iven that the farthest you can ever be from the sea in New Zealand is only something like 130km (in fact, it is the residents of Garston, Southland, who have to drive the furthest for a day at the beach), and that the great majority of Kiwis live little more than 10km from the coast, then it's only natural that the beach should assume such a large role here.

Add to the above a rich profusion of excellent beaches and bays around the coastline and it's little wonder that the summer holidays see a lemming-like migration from our cities and towns. From their suburban homes New Zealanders generally head east and west to settle themselves along the coast like so many migratory birds, making their temporary homes in tents, caravans and baches. For a society already greatly egalitarian, the beach is the final levelling, where labourers and executives, farming folk and townies blend in a confusion of jandals, shorts and t-shirts.

Symbolic of the beach and coastal New Zealand is the pohutukawa (*Metrosideros excelsa*), an enduring symbol of the New Zealand summer. Thriving on the salt spray and able to grow in the most difficult of sites, the pohutukawa, with its spreading limbs and often twisted trunks and roots, clothes cliff edges and beach fronts around the upper North Island.

The pohutukawa is commonly called the New Zealand Christmas Tree for its habit of flowering through December. It must have seemed reassuring during those first Christmases spent here by early European settlers, absent from the northern hemisphere's traditional green yuletide tree with its red trimming, to find the effect echoed here each December as pohutukawa lit up the coastline.

A New Zealand icon, the godwit is considered the most important of the migrant wading birds that fly to New Zealand's shores. Returning here each spring to over-winter far from their breeding grounds in northern Asia and Alaska, these waders congregate on the inter-tidal mudflats of a number of the country's harbours and estuaries. Although the total number of migrant species is around 40, the great majority of birds comprise godwit and knot species. The godwit population of around 100,000 is thought to make up the bulk of its breeding population.

The annual migration of these birds involves flights of tens of thousands of kilometres to and from their breeding grounds in Siberia and Alaska. New Zealand is the farthest south that waders in this region migrate, with only a small proportion of the populations of most species reaching here, the majority spending the southern summer in Australia. And the distances are huge: according to one expert, by the age of 17 an average wading bird will have flown more than 400,000km, further than the distance from the earth to the moon.

The route travelled is known as the East-Asia Australasian flyway, a route that takes the birds across Indonesia, Japan and China during a period of six to seven weeks and involves periods of flying of up to 5000km between stops.

The trip is done in stages, with the birds spending several weeks resting and feeding at stop-overs at sites in northern Australia and Asia. Leaving the northern breeding grounds in July, the birds reach New Zealand from late September. After moulting and intensive feeding over the summer to build up energy reserves, the birds fly away again from March.

Of the many roosting places in New Zealand, one of the most significant is Miranda in the Firth of Thames, near Auckland, which is the destination for many of the country's internal migrants as well, in particular the endemic wrybill.

The first people to provide a name for this country were the original settlers who arrived here from east Polynesia around 1000AD. Ancestors of the Maori, it is believed they applied the name Aotearoa, which translates literally as 'land of the long twilight'. The name, arguably, reflected the longer evenings the Polynesian settlers encountered in the southern Pacific. However, it seems that the concept of 'Aotearoa' later faded, to be revived at the end of the nineteenth century by a European appetite for ancient myths and legends. An alternative and more popular translation of Aotearoa as 'land of the long white cloud' probably dates from this period as well.

As for the country's two main islands, the Maori already had names for these: Te Ika a Maui, relating to the story of the country being hauled from the sea by Maui, and Te Ika a Pounamu, reflecting that island's resource of treasured greenstone. The third and most southern island was known as Te Puka-o-te-waka-a Maui, referring to the anchor stone of Maui's canoe.

Europeans eventually discovered and named New Zealand when, in 1642, Dutchman Abel Tasman reported '. . . a large land, uplifted high'. He was the first to chart it, although he did think that it was the west coast of a great southern continent. One hundred and thirty years later, James Cook became the first European to circumnavigate New Zealand and map its essential shape. There were a few excusable errors: Bank's Peninsula was believed to be an island, and Stewart Island was named Cape South and tentatively attached to the mainland. By 1841, in one of its first detailed maps, New Zealand had gained its now familiar shape, but with some notable differences in names. The North, South and Stewart Islands were respectively known as New Ulster, New Munster (or Middle Island) and New Leinster (or South Island).

Tasman believed that the coastline he'd sighted was connected with a great southern continent, linked to what the Dutch had already mapped at the southern end of South America, which they'd named Staten Landt. So this same name was given to Tasman's landfall. Later, in the second half of the seventeenth century, when it had become apparent that the coast Tasman had sighted was something else, the name was changed on Dutch maps to Nieuw Zeeland, in honour of the Dutch province of Zeeland, a province important to the Dutch East India Company which was sponsoring exploration at that time.

The ornithological oddity known as the kiwi has given this country a sense of identity, and been enthusiastically adopted as a national symbol.

New Zealanders of a century ago enjoyed a variety of monikers, being known variously as Maorilanders, En Zedders and Fernlanders. This apparent confusion was sorted out in the years following World War I, when the popularity of the 'Kiwi' brand of boot polish with troops in Europe inevitably led to the association of the bird with New Zealanders. And eventually the bird emerged as unchallenged — and unofficial — national symbol, outstripping other contenders such as the silver fern, moa and tui.

The kiwi's elevation as a symbol was enhanced by its reputation as something of an oddball. It may have been nocturnal, flightless and allegedly sightless, but was no slug on the ground and could defend itself when cornered. It was obviously a character, and one that was different. And as a symbol, it has demonstrated a remarkable durability.

The kiwi had enjoyed some 30 million years of relative peace before the arrival of humans in New Zealand. With no land mammals to speak of, it didn't even have to worry about its inability to fly. But human settlement brought with it a growing list of predators. In addition to cats and dogs, possums and stoats pose a serious threat to both the eggs and young of the kiwi. Recent studies suggest that kiwi populations on the North, South and Stewart Islands are halving every decade through land clearance and predation by introduced animals.

The kiwi is the most unlikely of birds. Flightless and nocturnal, it has a shaggy plumage that is more like hair than feathers. It is also the only bird to have nostrils at the end of its beak. In addition, its egg is bigger in proportion to body size than any other bird on earth. This curious biological trait may date from the kiwi's ancestral links with the giant moa and emu. For some reason the kiwi became smaller, but downsizing did not apply to its egg. But in spite of — or perhaps because of — all its oddities, the kiwi has been enthusiastically adopted by this country as its national symbol. And like the bird, New Zealand's geographic isolation has set the human Kiwis apart as original products of a unique country.

New Zealand was once described as consisting of two main islands separated by the Cook Strait Ferry. It could also be claimed that these two islands are held together by No.8 gauge fencing wire.

The conversion of this country's once plentiful bush cover into farmland began in the nineteenth century, creating a demand for good fences. These invariably consisted of posts set into the ground at regular intervals, and connected by three or four strands of wire stapled to battens. The preferred wire was known as No.8 gauge, galvanised and 4mm in diameter. Thousands of kilometres of this material encircle the farms and paddocks of New Zealand, but it was also put to other uses. A short length made a quick and effective replacement handle for a bucket, for example, and combined with pieces of 4x2 timber there wasn't much a handy farmer couldn't make or mend. No.8 has come to represent this nation's alleged ability to improvise, and make do with available resources.

New Zealanders certainly don't have a monopoly on ingenuity and invention — other countries have their Rube Goldbergs and their Heath-Robinsons — but perhaps the difference has been the degree to which the No.8 wire factor has permeated society here. While clichéd, it is true that Kiwis have been responsible for numerous important world-first developments and inventions. If not all have been entirely original, it has been the New Zealand way of looking at things that realised the idea's potential, a bit of native lateral thinking.

The usual explanation is that kiwi ingenuity was born of distance and isolation. Nineteenth-century European emigrants bound for New Zealand literally went to the ends of the earth, and months at sea provided essential training for the deprivations ahead. Once ashore, the new New Zealander often had to make do with what was at hand.

It is claimed that New Zealand inventiveness is becoming a thing of the past. If so, our changing lifestyle is probably to blame, in particular the move to smaller houses and apartments without back sheds or space for essential tinkering. The increasingly electronic world is denying people the satisfaction of making things by hand, and there are fewer items around the home that can now be fixed by pieces of No.8 wire.

When it comes to icons of local popular culture, the Buzzy Bee has dominated the field.

The inspired creation of brothers Hector (Hec) and John Ramsay, the Buzzy Bee has endeared itself to generations of New Zealanders. An intriguing concoction of clackety-clack sound, quivering antennae, spinning wings and bold colours, this delightful pull-along toy has been produced in the hundreds of thousands since its release in the 1940s.

As an extension of his Auckland woodturning business, Hec Ramsay made his first venture into toys with the famous Mary Lou doll in 1941. This wooden doll was an immediate hit, with thousands of little Kiwis cutting their teeth on its beaded limbs. Other wooden character toys followed, including the pull-along Richard Rabbit, Oscar Ostrich and Dorable Duck.

At the end of the Second World War, Hec was joined by his brother John, and it was John who would design their most famous toy of all, Buzzy Bee.

While Buzzy Bee has seen a number of design changes over the years since (the original cardboard wings, for example, which tended to suffer at the teeth of young children, were replaced with plastic ones), Buzzy Bee in late middle age is little altered.

The true origins of Buzzy Bee have always been a little hazy. There has long been the thought that Buzzy Bee has an American connection — if not ancestry. It may well be that its inspiration was a pull-along toy made by the Fisher-Price toy company. That company began life in 1930 and was well known for its own line of pull-along toys, including a bee. The real story of the origins of the New Zealand bee may lie deep in the archives of Fisher-Price.

Farm workers come four-legged as well as two, and the country's working dogs – from huntaways to strong-eyed and heading dogs – comprise a total population of around 140,000, most of them bred from collies.

These canine employees have the job of helping drove and pen the country's 40 million sheep and the skills they learn on the job find a competitive element each year in dog trials. Here the dogs get their chance to show what they can do when it comes to putting the sheep into mobs and then controlling them into pens.

An undoubted downside of being a working dog in New Zealand is the frequent dosing against hydatid tapeworms that can plague a canine. In New Zealand the dog is the only animal capable of carrying the hydatid tapeworm. To protect farm stock, humans and the meat industry from possible infection it is important to break the cycle between infected sheep and dogs. To this end dogs are regularly purged at dog-dosing strips.

The most famous of the country's sheepdogs is 'Dog', the hero of local cartoon strip *Footrot Flats*. The creation of cartoonist Murray Ball, *Footrot Flats* was first published here in 1975. With what has been described as an appeal to 'cowpat patriotism', the strip and its characters – Dog, Wal, Cooch and company – has been a spectacular success that has spawned books, a film and even a stage show. All thanks to a recipe that blends the realities and fantasies of rural life with a dog struggling to make sense out of it all.

New Zealanders love their ice cream and Kiwis have established themselves at number three in the world rankings of ice cream eaters. At the same time they have also boosted the reputation of the local Tip Top brand.

Today's ice cream giant had a classic humble start, in the shape of the Royal ice cream company in Dunedin. In the early 1930s the then manager of Royal and one of his customers decided to go into the ice cream business for themselves. Armed with their own ice cream recipe and leased premises in Wellington, the two partners began to offer the public a new type of shop selling solely ice creams and milkshakes. It was the country's very first milkbar.

In search of a name for their new enterprise, the two partners were seated in a restaurant when they overheard a fellow diner use the then common expression 'tip top!' in his praise of the restaurant's service. The two partners had their name and a legend was born.

The country's first ice cream had been hand-churned and sold from handcarts, but as milkbars became popular, much of the country's ice cream was manufactured on the premises, with the ice cream sold over the counter. If it had a brand name at all, it took the name of the milkbar. When ice cream making became mechanised and was removed to separate factories, many of the original brand names were carried over: such evocative names as Everest, Sunshine, Blue Bell, Arctic,

Egmont, Peter Pan, Alpine, Frosty Jack and Glacier.

A favourite Tip Top flavour is hokey-pokey, a blend of vanilla base with pieces of toffee, introduced into its range in the 1950s. While the idea of adding toffee to ice cream wasn't new, what is unique is the taste imparted by hokey-pokey toffee. The toffee was formed in large sheets which were then broken up with hammers and the smaller pieces distributed into the vanilla base. However, irregular-sized and -shaped pieces of the toffee would cause occasional jamming of the machinery, and today's requirement for high-volume production has seen the toffee manufactured in standardised pellets.

Three species of paua are found in New Zealand, including *Haliotis iris*, the common paua and probably the most familiar of all New Zealand shells. Found only in the seas around New Zealand, the common paua is a species of abalone.

The shell's mother-of-pearl iridescent colouring can be seen in greens, blues, purples and pinks. These marvellous hues are affected to a degree by the animal's eating habits, with, for example, striking blue-green produced in those areas where the paua feed mainly on brown kelp. The black 'contour-line' patterns are formed as layers of protein are laid down between the layers of calcium that go to form the shell.

Paua flesh was used by Maori for food, and its shell as decoration in carvings. The shell has also for a long time found use in souvenirs and fishing lures. More recently, increasing use is being made of the iridescent shell to provide accents to furniture designs and in artworks. Perhaps the most famous use of the shell is the Paua Shell House in Bluff in which the living-room walls are covered with polished whole paua shells.

The paua lives in shallow waters, and the dull, often encrusted outer surface of the shell can easily be missed. The row of holes in the shell are for the expulsion of used water processed by the animal's gills. The black meat of the animal is prized as a delicacy.

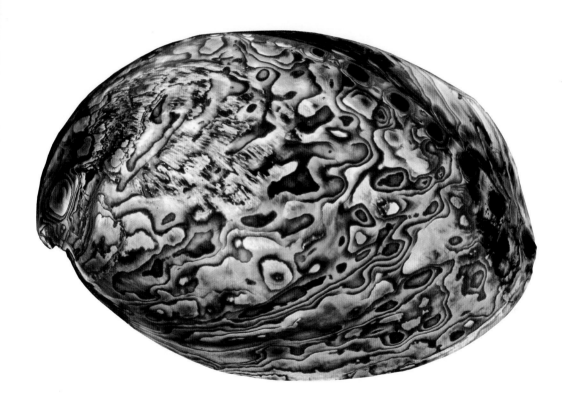

'*It must be Wattie's!*' This line from the old jingle symbolises the vision James Wattie had for the company that bears his name. It was during the early 1930s that James Wattie first became aware of the opportunity for a local cannery. Each summer in his home province of Hawke's Bay the huge fruit and vegetable surplus of this productive region would literally rot on the ground while the country continued to import canned product.

Wattie had a vision of a New Zealand self-sufficient in canned fruit and vegetables and his venture was a success from the outset, creating thousands of jobs. The crops that grew in Hawke's Bay's fertile Heretaunga Plains soon gave the province the name of 'the fruit bowl of New Zealand'.

Over the years, canned peaches, tomato sauce, peas, baked beans, asparagus and fruit salad came to be synonymous with the Wattie's name. And under James Wattie's direction the situation that had existed in the early 1930s, when 80 per cent of the country's canned foods were imported, was turned around. In fact, when he retired some forty years later the country had not only become self-sufficient but was now a major exporter of such canned foods. Reflecting the degree to which Wattie's had become a part of popular life, a university revue of the time could include a song – to the tune of 'Land of Hope and Glory' – that went: *Land of fern and paua / Nestled by the sea / Peaches, peas and baked beans / Canned by James Wattie!*

Wattie's

GREEN PEAS

Cabbage Tree

One of the most distinctive features of the New Zealand landscape are the Dr Seuss-like forms of the cabbage tree — (*Cordyline australis*), topped with their crowns of spiky leaves. New Zealand is home to four species of *Cordyline*, *C. australis* being the best known.

The common name 'cabbage' is something of a misnomer, and was given to the tree by European explorers not in relation to the appearance of the cabbage-like crown of leaves, but rather as the general name then applied to palm trees. Early explorers here confused the *Cordyline* with other true palms such as the nikau. Parts of the bushy leaf crowns were eaten, however. While the outer part is extremely tough and bitter, the pith and inner roots were eaten by Maori, who knew the tree as the *ti*.

Cabbage trees can grow as tall as 20 metres and inhabit forest margins, river banks, clearings and swamps throughout the country. They have many relatives overseas, including yuccas and Joshua trees in the Americas. The cabbage tree was once hailed as the largest lily in the world, but can no longer make this claim as it is not now classified as a member of the lily family. However, as some sort of compensation, it may be one of the largest agave trees.

In recent years the cabbage tree population has been struck by a disease which has also spread to other native trees and plant crops. The problem is a bacterium carried by an insect, and compounded by changes to the tree's natural environment. As New Zealand's swampland disappears, so too does its once common symbol, the cabbage tree.

The typical New Zealand house has a wrinkled iron roof, a system preferred here since the late 1840s. In England, corrugated iron was only considered suitable for temporary structures and fences, but New Zealand builders had no such reservations. They quickly found it provided a simple and efficient covering for roofs and chimneys. Initially imported, the iron was first manufactured in this country in 1869, and the galvanising process for extra rust resistance began here in 1886. As roofing, it was usually painted a red iron oxide, or a more fade-proof 'permanent' green.

The versatile corrugated iron has also been used for fences, woolsheds, water tanks and dog kennels, creating what writer Geoff Chapple has described as an 'unremitting ripple' across the land. Along with 4x2 (now 100x50) framing and weatherboards, corrugated iron is the great New Zealand building material. If it was considered inferior back in England, New Zealand has taken it to new heights. In this regard, the last word belongs to artist Jeff Thomson, who has used corrugated iron to produce a menagerie of remarkable animals and, most famously, clad the outside of an automobile or two.

Less well-known is the material's role in the splitting of the atom, for it was in a two-storey corrugated-iron shed at the University of Canterbury that Ernest Rutherford, later Lord Rutherford and New Zealand's most famous scientist, learnt his chemistry. Rutherford's work in nuclear physics led to the atomic age, following his theorising that the atom was made up of smaller components — later proved by the so-called splitting of the atom in a proton accelerator.

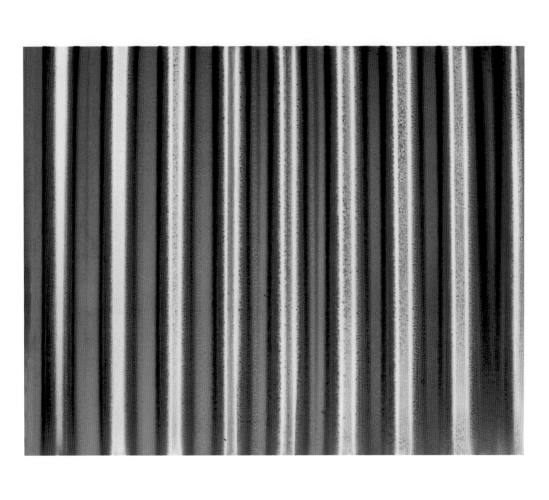

One of New Zealand's best-known and most durable commercial trademarks was born in 1879 when, determined to boost trade in his Lyttelton grocer's shop, Thomas Edmonds decided to manufacture and sell his own brand of baking powder. When a doubting customer asked if it would work, Edmonds assured her that her scones were indeed 'sure to rise'. Thus inspired, he designed his now famous rising sun label and went into business. A trial run of 200 tins proved successful, and soon all of Canterbury seemed to be baking with his powder.

Word spread and it became the national favourite, and in 1912 annual sales of tins passed the magic one million mark. Three years later annual sales were equivalent to six-and-a-half tins for every family in the Dominion, and by 1928 the 2,500,000 mark was passed.

Meanwhile, in 1907, Edmonds published the first edition of its *Cookery Book* with 'economical everyday recipes and cooking hints', most of which required a certain brand of baking powder. Still going, although updated and now cooking with gas and microwave, *The Edmonds Cookery Book* is New Zealand's best-selling book ever.

In addition to cookery requisites, Thomas Edmonds also gave the city of Christchurch a clock tower and band rotunda to mark his 50 years of business in 1929. His Ferry Road factory was famous for its award-winning gardens. That factory is no more, however, and the baking powder is now made in Auckland.

While New Zealanders no longer bake as often as they used to, when they do they're still most likely to reach for the packet with the cheerful 'sure to rise' symbol.

F ew national symbols could claim to have begun as a doodle on a desk calendar, as did the Four Square device. And it was a square drawn around a certain date in July 1924 – the 4th – that was the inspiration for the Four Square name for a co-operative of grocery stores. Set up to counter the growing threat of chain stores, this new organisation already had 112 member stores by 1931.

In 1947 the general manager of Four Square went to America to investigate the new grocery concept of 'self-service', which was introduced to this country the following year. By 1950, Four Square could claim to be 'The Dominion's largest grocery chain' with 700 members, and within another six years it had passed the 1000 mark. By then it had also acquired its other distinctive image, the smiling grocer in his apron with a pencil behind his ear, ready to take the customer's order. This symbol was surreptitiously based on an actual Four Square grocer, unaware of his important role until many years later.

During the 1960s New Zealand grocers had to cope with the imminent arrival of another American idea, the supermarket. Four Square countered by encouraging speed and efficiency among its staff at annual conventions – 22 seconds being the record for 'checking out' 20 grocery items – and there were also 'Mini-for-Mum' competitions, and to celebrate the day that started it all, prizes for all New Zealand babies born on the 4th of July.

In 1956 the Japanese swimming team were observed wearing a new type of casual footwear at the Melbourne Olympic Games. Around the same time, Auckland businessman Morris Yock saw similar versions of traditional thongs on a visit to Asia and determined to introduce the idea to New Zealand.

The following year Morris' son Anthony went into production in a Te Papapa, Auckland, garage. Christening the new product 'Jandal' – inspired by 'Japanese sandal' – the first of these local thongs, in brown and white, were punched out of rubber sheets brought from Hong Kong. However, difficulties in importing the rubber saw Skellerup Industries Ltd of Christchurch take over the supply of materials, eventually buying the Jandal brand and business altogether.

The next few decades were a golden age for the jandal, but in the 1990s it began to face competition from imported look-alikes. When some of these competing products began making use of Jandal, a registered trade name, as a generic term, the owners of the original Jandal threatened legal action. Meanwhile, the genuine item could be distinguished from the competition by its solid rubber construction and lack of fancy fabric tops, toe grooves and bright colours. Ironically, the genuine jandal is now an import itself, being made in Malaysia.

In more recent years, the thong market has declined as a result of the rise of the sports sandal. However, after 44 years of service the original Jandal remains a steady seller – particularly in denim blue and silver.

One of New Zealand's most famous products had ignominious beginnings in a Paeroa cow paddock. It was around the end of the nineteenth century that local residents were first aware of a natural spring that produced a refreshing drink, especially if a slice or two of lemon was added. Sensing the commercial potential the Paeroa Natural Mineral Water Company began bottling operations in the town, although at first the drink was promoted for its therapeutic rather than thirst-quenching properties.

In 1907 cordial manufacturers Menzies & Co bought the business and began shipping casks of mineral water to its factory in Auckland's Eden Crescent. Presumably following local advice they began adding lemon, and what was initially known as 'Paeroa and Lemon' was born.

Transporting casks to Auckland was an expensive business and eventually, following the analysis of the Paeroa water (the analysis revealed various salts such as magnesium carbonate which if added to pure water produced a result indistinguishable from the real thing), manufacturing was moved to Auckland. For this reason the drink, now known as Lemon and Paeroa, or just L&P, is officially described as a 'sparkling' as opposed to 'natural' mineral water.

In 1969 Paeroa's contribution to refreshment was celebrated in the form of a 7-metre tall bottle, erected at the intersection of State Highways 2 and 26. In recent years, thanks to a quirky advertising campaign, the drink has garnered an increasing number of drinkers drawn to its 'world famous in New Zealand' branding.

In the days when cars were relative luxuries, New Zealanders tended to take the train. The New Zealand Railways thoughtfully provided refreshment stops where hungry passengers could stock up on sandwiches, pies and cups of tea. Mostly these stops were only long enough for queuing – the eating and drinking had to be done on board.

And if the food was unremarkable, it was at least distinguished by the crockery, made by the Amalgamated Brick and Tile Company of Auckland. Originally established to produce sewer pipes and electrical porcelains, during the Second World War the company had diversified to produce crockery for the American Navy stationed in this country. In 1943 another order for crockery came, this time from the New Zealand Railways. Their new cups proved virtually indestructible, and needed to be when they were collected up later on board by guards who moved through the carriages with wire baskets and kerosene tin boxes.

Legendary among the refreshment stops was that in Taumarunui, whose canteen was immortalised in a song by writer Peter Cape. 'Taumarunui on The Main Trunk Line' tells the story of a passenger who, in love with a woman in the canteen, gets a job as a fireman on the Limited Express night train in order to see her. Alas, his 'sheila' switches to the day shift.

In 1948 the department of Amalgamated Brick and Tile responsible for making the crockery became a separate company, known as Crown Lynn and specialising in domestic and art crockery. Among its best-known products were kiwi and swan vases, which took up residency on many of the nation's window sills and mantelpieces.

The Taumarunui stop ceased in 1975 when the canteen dispensed its last pie and cup of tea. Fourteen years later, succumbing to the increasing flood of imported pottery lines, Crown Lynn also closed its doors.

Silver Fern

When New Zealand was in need of a national symbol in the late nineteenth century there were two obvious contenders. One of these, the fern, was such a predominant feature of the local bush that this country was at that time popularly referred to as Fernland.

A member of the common tree fern family generally known as ponga, the silver fern is distinguished by dark green foliage on its upper surfaces and intense silver colouring below. As a symbol it has found wide-ranging application on a host of New Zealand products including butter, cheese and tobacco labels. Worn on the jerseys of the New Zealand Native rugby team that toured Britain in 1888, it has been used — a silver or white fern design on a black ground — as this country's main sporting emblem ever since.

In 1956 the silver fern was incorporated into the revised New Zealand Coat of Arms, and so now enjoyed official status. In this respect it had an advantage over its traditional rival for national symbol, the kiwi. The flightless bird has never received official recognition, but may take some satisfaction from the fact that New Zealanders are now known as Kiwis. Meanwhile, the silver fern continues to appear (along with sponsors' symbols) on the All Blacks jersey. For a while it also inspired a railcar on the Main Trunk Line, and it remains the name of the national netball team.

Historically, the New Zealand wardrobe has been highly practical. Along with gumboots and black bush singlets there is of course the Swanndri shirt.

Traditionally New Zealand's favourite outdoor shirt, the Swanndri has its origins in 1914 when William Henry Broome registered a distinctive swan trademark for a line of ready-made clothing. He also managed a curious spelling of his chosen brand name, a combination of the words 'swan' and 'dry' that would imply waterproof. In 1937 tailor John McKendrick became involved in the business, and produced a rugged woollen garment that set the pattern for the now famous Swanndri shirt.

The earliest of these were knee-length and single-coloured — typically dark green — and often had a hood. Of pure wool, the shirts were eventually produced in a range of checks and plain shades, and proved ideal for bushworkers and farmers who appreciated their warmth and shower-proof qualities. Before long the Swanndri had become an essential part of New Zealand's outdoor wardrobe, standard dress for farmers, fishermen, contractors, power supply workers and the armed forces.

In recent years the Swanndri — more usually referred to as the swanni, swannie or swanny — has drifted away from its traditional dependence on the rural sector to appeal to the urban and tourist markets as well. Frequently worn with jeans and gumboots, or boots and balaclava, the swanni is now also available in a summer weight and looks forward to becoming a fashionable year-round garment.

Swanndri garments were once made in the Taranaki town of Waitara, and are now manufactured at the Alliance Textiles mill in Timaru, South Canterbury.

The finest expression of kiwi ingenuity also happens to be one of the simplest. The home-made Taranaki gate symbolises rural inventiveness and the ability to make do. It is made of wire (either No. 8 or barbed) stapled to battens and strung between two strainer posts to which it is attached with loops of (No. 8) wire. When the top loop is lifted, the tension is released and the gate can be 'opened'.

The advantages of the Taranaki gate are its cheapness — being able to be made on site using local materials and tools — and its adaptability to sloping country and to both wide and narrow gateways. Further, it can be 'locked', is suitable for all types of stock, and is long-lasting and easily repaired.

Correctly or otherwise, such improvised gates — of which there are various types — are attributed to Taranaki and have been known by this name since at least the 1930s. It is possible that the name was originally intended to be less than complimentary. Despite this the region may well be happy to take credit for the gate, as it does for certain other curious rural terms that now enrich the national dictionary. These include 'Taranaki sunshine', meaning rain or drizzle, and 'Taranaki top-dressing', which refers to cow manure lying in its naturally deposited state. Such ironic expressions are said to reflect the tough times experienced by Taranaki farmers in the 1920s and 1930s. Rough-and-ready solutions were called for, and farmers became adept at recycling, even giving old rabbit traps and lengths of dog chain another life. But of all their improvised solutions, there was surely none better, or more celebrated, than the Taranaki gate.

The Sanitarium Health Food Company originated in Michigan, USA, and has been practising its 'Health is Wealth' maxim in New Zealand since 1898. In 1930 Sanitarium purchased the Christchurch company Grain Products Ltd and thereby became the owner of a flake biscuit named Weet-Bix, which has gone on to capture some 40 per cent of the nation's breakfast cereal market.

And Weet-Bix has proved as versatile as it is popular and can be eaten with hot or cold milk, depending on the time of year, or simply spread with jam or Marmite. As 'the perfect winter breakfast' it had the distinction of being chosen by Sir Edmund Hillary for both his Mt Everest and Antarctic expeditions.

New Zealanders now consume a staggering 312 million Weet-Bix every year. For an idea of how many this is, imagine these Weet-Bix laid end to end in a straight line and then driving alongside that line at 100kph day and night. It would be 13 days before you passed the last Weet-Bix.

The cereal also provides young New Zealanders with a regular source of general knowledge. Since 1941 Weet-Bix packets have included free full-colour cards on a wide range of subjects, beginning with 'The Treasury of the Years' series. These cards have proved extremely collectable, and Sanitarium continues to issue an average of two series per year.

Some people eat Weet-Bix for lunch and dinner as well as breakfast and New Zealand is rich in tales of extraordinary consumption. Included in the annals of what is a cereal subculture are attempts on the record for the most Weet-Bix at a sitting. Currently this stands at around 38 Weet-Bix (with milk) inside of 40 minutes.

In further honouring the national breakfast, 'Weet-Bix' is the name mountaineers give to a certain type of loose shattered rock.

It could be claimed that New Zealand's national colour is black. This apparent preference for what is defined as the absence of colour dates back to the jerseys (and shorts) used by New Zealand's national rugby teams of the 1880s, and adopted by the original All Blacks of 1905. It is generally accepted, however, that the nation's first fifteen were named, not for the colour of the team's jerseys, but as a result of a typographical mistake, when 'All Backs' appeared in the British press as 'All Blacks'. Nevertheless, the name stuck and that colour has since been adopted by many of New Zealand's other sporting codes.

Black seemed the ideal colour for our rugby team, going about its business with grim determination. The black concept gained a further dimension during New Zealand's bid for the America's Cup in the 1980s. Our boat was named *Black Magic*, and became the subject of intense patriotic fervour. Around the same time, black acquired the added distinction of being a fashionable colour. Although not something that would have bothered the All Blacks a decade or so earlier, it no doubt befitted their new professional image.

There is always the possibility that New Zealand's preoccupation with black reflects something dark and gloomy within the national psyche. Equally, however, it is probably historical: singleted farmers and bushmen were wearing black long before it became fashionable. Their preferred colour is an extremely sensible one for muddy conditions — both on and off the field.

Once the motorcar had opened up otherwise inaccessible parts of the coast to holiday-makers, New Zealanders were able to establish and enjoy that little slice of heaven by the sea called the bach.

The history of New Zealand's baches is a rich tale of recycling and building in peculiar places. Many of the first baches were built from the likes of used car cases made of durable hardwoods like cedar. Old trams have also been put to good use, as has the occasional cave. Classic construction materials also include fibrolite and board-and-batten.

Through until the late 1960s the humble bach mushroomed along the country's coastline. In the years since, the demand for a slice of coastal living in those areas within a comfortable drive of the main cities has seen the bach become a luxury now unaffordable to the average worker. At the same time the once-humble bolt-hole is increasingly being replaced by the kind of houses, replete with mod cons, we were once happy to leave in town.

The bach's original philosophy was simplicity, and was an eagerly anticipated contrast with home life. Here, meals were fairly informal and nobody got into too much trouble for bringing sand inside. Some baches may have bordered on the primitive, but that was their charm. Certainly – in earlier days anyway – there seemed little point in the slavish duplication of city domesticity at the beach. And the bach therefore became a handy retirement home for furniture and fittings that had already done their dash.

What is 'bach' in the North Island, in the South Island becomes 'crib', although this perhaps more particularly describes a river or mountain holiday house.

Classic Kiwiana